Deep Learning
Step-by-Step

*A Sensible Guide Presenting the Concepts of
Deep Learning with Real World Examples*

Matthew Harper

Table of Contents

Introduction

Congratulations on downloading *Deep Learning Step-by-Step* and thank you for doing so.

If you are new to the concept of deep learning, you might assume that it is some fundamental of education, a better way to teach in the classroom. Something along the lines of a new and innovative way to get students to absorb more information. If you have some foundation in computer science, then you would have a general idea of what it really is. While you would be wrong on the first assumption, you would still be close to grasping the basic idea of deep learning. However, there is one fundamental difference that makes it unique.

Deep learning is not about people, but instead, a method of machine learning. Yes, the machines are actually the students in this concept. It is a learning system that uses algorithms that have been developed that attempts to mimic the human brain and the way it gathers information, analyzes, and makes decisions based on the data received. In essence, through the use of these algorithms, deep learning makes it possible for machines to absorb new information and to apply it to their functions.

It helps to understand a little about the human brain functions to help us see how deep learning actually works. For thousands of years, the human brain has been the hallmark of intelligent life. No other creature on the planet has come close to having the capacity of the human brain. Its ability to capture millions of bits of information through its senses, process it, reason on it, store information, and dictate to the body exactly how it should respond has mystified scientists for eons. For the layperson, it can be quite difficult to see exactly how machine learning could possibly have the ability to do the same thing.

There are quite a few similarities that machines now have in common with the human brain as well as differences. Understanding the way learning happens naturally can help us to understand how a machine can be programmed to learn in this phenomenal new type of technology.

In the human brain, learning stems from its millions of interconnected neurons. These could be likened to the tiny connections you might find in a spider web but with an amazing difference. When the brain is exposed to some form of stimulation, these neurons instinctively adjust to the new information by changing their configuration. With each change, new connections are formed, old ones are strengthened, and those that have not been used for a long time are eliminated. This is why the more one completes a task, the better they get at it.

Think about this, if you are learning to play the piano, the first time you touch the keys your performance will be clumsy and awkward. You are unsure of where the keys are, which ones to hit, and how long to hold each note, and how the note will harmonize with the one before it or after it. But if you make it a habit to practice regularly, you'll find that you will eventually approach the keyboard and play songs, notes, and tunes without even thinking about it. The neurons that fired when you were practicing will have become very strong from repeated use.

If you continue to practice, eventually you could become a master pianist.

Our neurons are capable of processing all sorts of stimuli by utilizing tools from our memory and our perceptions at the time. Each time it receives stimuli through our five senses, a different subset of our enormous supply of neurons is triggered creating knowledge.

Neuroscience (or the study of the brain) is the biological pattern from which deep learning has been created. The networks that process deep learning have been labeled as "artificial neural networks" or ANN because they are designed to mimic the same neural pathways of the human brain. While a neural network cannot exactly replicate the amazing ability of the human brain, the general concept is very similar. Throughout the pages of this book, we will break down the complex design of these artificial neural networks (ANN) so you can better grasp what deep learning is and the myriad of ways it can be used.

There are plenty of books on this subject on the market, thanks again for choosing this one! Every effort was made to ensure it is full of as much useful information as possible, please enjoy!

Chapter 1:
A Brief Overview of Deep Learning

Deep learning has probably become one of the most complex developments that mankind has created to date. Scientists have gone far beyond simply creating machines that can learn and have gone on to focus on other advances that will make the technology we have now ancient seem like ancient history before the majority of us ever have the chance to fully grasp it.

Why Do We Need it?

There are millions of different uses for deep learning, most of them probably haven't been thought of yet but its practical applications even today have already proved to be revolutionary in their ability to simplify our world around us.

No doubt, for the average person, the idea can be extremely intimidating, but reality tells us that its implementation in our daily lives will only continue to grow. It is already being used in space for special projects like the Google Brain, and DeepMind. It is the technology that anticipates what movies you will watch next on Netflix, which is the same technology that determines what advertisements flash before your eyes when you're searching the Internet.

The fact is that deep learning is one of the few methods that allow us to get around many challenges. It makes it possible to have a machine focus on certain elements in a situation or environment without being programmed to do so. Still, it is very easy to see how machine learning is needed today. Even now, machines that can do deep learning are able to master certain skills that before only humans could do.

For example, these machines can recognize patterns. They can decipher facial identities and facial expressions. This can help in protecting us from identity theft and a host of other criminal activities. They can even identify speech patterns so that the way we speak can be used to identify us in much the same way as our fingerprints or our DNA are already used. The benefits of this alone are phenomenal.

Deep learning also helps machines to recognize various anomalies. Financial institutions are already using them to identify unusual sequences that are out of the norm when purchases or made. Nuclear power plants use them to monitor sensor readings, so they can determine the potential for a critical event long before it becomes a danger.

Deep learning can be used in making more accurate predictions, so we can better plan for the future. Whether it is weather changes or fluctuations in stock prices, knowing what is more likely to happen tomorrow, next month or next year are important factors that can help us make many important decisions in our life; this ability can find practical uses in all sorts of industries. Imagine what can be done in genetics, in health, in science, in manufacturing, and in a host of other fields we all rely on.

While machines are still a long way from matching perfectly the tasks that the human brain can do, the use of deep learning can definitely usher us into a whole new way of learning that goes beyond the simplistic abilities they have had in the past. Only time will tell what deep learning will provide us within the coming years.

History of Deep Learning

A mere five years ago, the concept of deep learning was mostly relegated to be a niche field of interest. It was far from a programming method adopted by the mainstream population. But in that very short period of time, there has been a marked increase in this type of machine learning. If you've been connected in the computer science fields for any length of time, you've probably already noticed that research on the subject has been repeatedly recorded in computer journals like Science Nature, JAMA, and Nature Methods. Even if you're not in the field of science, you've no doubt heard about the Smart Cars that can drive themselves, the computer that was able to copy a masterpiece painting, or even their ability to diagnose major health diseases.

Even with all the hype and excitement around it today, it is interesting to note that the main idea behind deep learning has been in place for decades. However, this global fascination with the machine learning couldn't fully materialize until computers had the ability to work at speeds fast enough to make it possible to tap into the true power behind it. There have been several milestones that have been instrumental in putting deep learning on the global scientific map, let's take a look at some of them.

Early in the 1940s, during the heart of World War II, the concept of a thinking machine was first introduced. It was first mentioned in a seminal paper by Alan Turing, *Computing Machinery and Intelligence.* In his paper, Turing points out several very specific criteria that would determine whether or not it was even possible for a computer to be intelligent. The criteria eventually became known as the 'Turing test.'

- **Electronic Brain – 1943**

  In those days, machine learning was limited because our understanding of the human brain was far from accurate. The first to work on the concept of an electronic brain were two scientists by the names of Walter Pitts and Warren McCulloch who developed a technique called the "threshold logic unit," which was designed to mimic the way people thought a neuron worked in a real brain. It was dubbed "the electronic brain."

- **Perceptron – 1957**

  This idea had its limits since an accurate understanding of how the brain worked had yet to be discovered. The concept of a thinking machine was stalled until Frank Rosenblatt introduced a program called, "Perceptron" in 1957. This turned out to be the precursor for the modern neural networks we use today. Perceptron, for its time, was an amazing discovery. Considered to be the "embryo of an electronic computer," it was expected to allow machines to be able to walk, talk, see, and write in pretty much the same way as humans would. It gave machines the ability to recognize and identify letters and numbers and was believed that in time, a machine programmed with perceptron would be able to reproduce and be aware of its own existence. This was the first time we were to hear the words "Artificial Intelligence."

Perceptron had its own limitations though. As it began to generate growing interest in the scientific community, those limitations became very evident. As they noticed, these machines could differentiate between numbers and letters, the results were not consistent. It could recognize an E from an F or a 5 from a 6, but if other stimuli were found near or around the figures it was trying to read, the machine's ability to identify what it was seeing literally fell apart. The problem became known as the XOr Problem.

The conclusion that resulted was that many determined it to be impossible for a machine to learn regardless of how much time was invested in training it. This belief virtually put the idea of perceptron as the birth of the neural net on hold indefinitely.

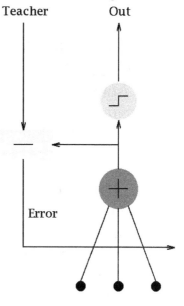

- **ADALINE/MADELINE – 1960**

Soon after, ADALINE was introduced by Bernard Widrow. Similar to perceptron, it used a threshold logic device designed to perform a linear summation of inputs and then classify them into different patterns. The algorithm used for Adaline was a learning control mechanism that took various input data, analyzed it and made comparisons, and then generated specific outputs.

Adaline had a 5-step learning procedure:

o Set all weights and thresholds to small bipolar random values

o Introduce new inputs along with the desired outputs

o Calculate the actual outputs

o Adapt the weights

o Repeat steps two to four until the desired outputs and the actual outputs are equal

While Adaline had the same basic neural structure as Perceptron had, it was found that it could only distinguish linearly separable patterns. This made it one step closer to future artificial intelligence, but it was still short of the ultimate goal.

Another system created about the same time was MADELINE, which used numerous adaptive linear neurons, but they were arranged in a multilayer network. This type of program used a majority vote rule on the outputs from the Adaline layer. In other words, if more than 50% of the outputs from Adaline were a +1 then the Madeline would also have an output of +1. This gave Madeline the ability to classify nonlinear functions that were similar to multi-layer Perceptron.

Madeline had a six-step learning procedure:

- o Initialize weights and thresholds

- o Present new inputs and desired outputs

- o Calculate the actual outputs

- o Determine the actual Madeline outputs

- o Determine error and update weights

- o Repeat steps two to five until the desired outputs and the actual outputs are equal for all vectors

- **Addressing the XOr Problem – 1969**

In time, perceptron began to attract a lot of attention again, especially by Marvin Minsky, who would later become the father of artificial intelligence. While on the surface the concept seemed good, Minsky was the one who detected problems with the program. His concern lied not in what the machine was able to do but instead of what it couldn't. While the machine could learn, it was incapable of learning the exclusive function or the XOr. Minsky also proved that not only could the machine NOT learn this function but that it was theoretically impossible to learn it.

To solve the problems, he proposed a new structure of the pattern of neural networks with a special output labeled as the "Reject output". This was meant to be used to separate out any patterns that the machine would have difficulty recognizing.

- **Multi-Layered Perceptron or Backpropagation – 1986**

  It took years for interest to build up again in the field. It wasn't until the 1980s that another spark of life began to emerge. A new individual entered the arena by the name of Geoff Hinton. He along with David Rumelhart and Ronald Williams published a paper, *"Learning representation by back-propagating errors."* Here they explained that it was possible for the numerous hidden layers of neural nets to be trained. The procedure was relatively simple; by using these hidden layers it was possible for these nets to bypass the weakness of perceptron. It appeared that they now had figured out a way to give the network the ability to learn nonlinear functions. In fact, it was also discovered that these networks could learn any function with these hidden layers.

  The algorithm was able to work by using the derivative of the networks' loss function and back-propagating the errors in order to update the parameters of the lower layers. The first attempts to try this algorithm were quite successful especially when it trained convolutional neural nets to recognize handwritten digits.

  However, as successful as it was in the early stages, their efforts were not able to yield the same results with larger problems, sending the concept into another deep freeze where research was all but stopped once again.

- **SVM – 1995**

A decade later, the 90s introduced the Support Vector Machine (SVM). This quickly became the preferred method of machine learning, which quickly sent the neural nets to the back of the line. It would be another decade and a half before they were able to be brought out again. The problem then was that their computing power was much too slow to do what they were attempting to do.

- **Deep Neural Network – 2006**

Around 2006, Hinton announced that he finally knew how the human brain really worked and introduced a new idea. The unsupervised pre-training and deep belief nets became the next advancement in machine learning. The concept was to train a restricted Boltzmann machine, an unsupervised model, to freeze all parameters. Then they would add a new layer over them and train only the parameters of the new layer. In that vein, they could continue adding and training layers until you had built up a deep network. Finally, they would use the result to initialize the parameters of the traditional neural network. With this strategy, they found it was possible to train networks that were much deeper than any other attempts they had previously made.

- **Breakthrough – 2012**

Now that interest was building up again, more people dove into the research. 2012 was the year that things literally began to take off for deep learning. They had begun to use these deep nets for speech recognition. It was the first time that a neural model had been able to be considered "state of the art."

However, more complications were in the future. As these neural nets began to surpass the more traditional methods used, things did not always pan out as they expected. The issue was addressed head-on in 2012 at the Large Scale Visual Recognition Challenge. This was a competition where challengers could build their own computer vision models, submit predictions, and be scored according to their accuracy. The first two years of the competition (2010, 2011), the top winners had error rates of 26 and 28%. However, in 2012, Geoff Hinton along with Alex Krizhevsky, and Ilya Sutskever submitted a model that yielded an error rate of only 16% literally blowing the competition out of the water.

How were they able to accomplish this? They used graphics processing units (GPUs) in their training approach. Because GPUs are basically parallel floating-point calculators with hundreds or thousands of cores, they were able to operate must faster allowing them to train larger models. This made it possible for them to achieve much lower error rates. In addition, they were able to introduce something called a dropout, which allowed them to lower their overfitting and use the rectified linear activation unit. Both of these became their main components for modern-day deep learning. Their network became known as Alexnet.

Alexnet ushered in a whole new era. After its introduction, many more new innovations have been introduced in rapid succession. It was the machine that finally gave deep learning its wings. Today, it is believed that we are on the very precipice of a full-scale artificial intelligence age. Nearly every industry in existence is shelling out billions of dollars on research and to acquire AI technology and the talent to run it. Right now, we are in a paradigm shift in machine learning and there is no turning back.

Chapter 2:
What You Need to Know to Get Started with Deep Learning

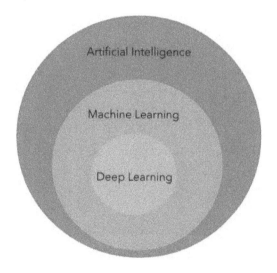

The innovations and breakthroughs that have been accomplished with deep learning are enough to get a lot of people excited about it. It is said that we live in the age of technology and with the many strides already achieved by deep learning, the next age will probably be the age of artificial intelligence. To that end, there will be more and more people looking to enter this field, so they can have a role in ushering in this new era.

However, before they can do that there are a lot of things you must come to understand. Now that these fundamentals are so clearly realized, we will begin to see artificial intelligence emerge in all sorts of industries. We've already discussed how it is being used in areas of pattern recognition, and object detection, but the extent of deep learning will one day go much further than that.

This is a complex field and for anyone to get a firm grasp on it, it helps to have a basic understanding of subjects like linear algebra, calculus, probability, and programming. This knowledge will be very beneficial in helping you to grasp the concepts we will be mentioning later in this book. If you don't have this background, it doesn't mean that you cannot grasp these concepts, but it does mean you'll have to do a little extra homework to get through the meat of it all.

You'll also need to know some practical differences in how deep learning differs and why it is so much more efficient than any other type of artificial intelligence before it.

Deep Learning, Machine Learning, Artificial Intelligence – What's the Difference?

Often when you research deep learning you'll come across several different terms that seem to be used interchangeably. Deep learning, machine learning, and artificial intelligence. While these are all related there are some distinct differences that set them all apart from each other.

So, what exactly is deep learning? Basically, it is a type of machine learning that uses a system of neural networks that are designed to mimic the learning of the human brain. This network's focus is to simplify how a machine uses certain learning algorithms, which can be applied in artificial intelligence and machine learning. In fact, it is virtually impossible to have artificial intelligence without deep learning.

Because of deep learning, we now have the ability to develop massively large neural networks that have the ability to absorb information and respond to it without the need for a human to program it's every move. The expectation is that one day, these machines will be able to operate autonomously, completely on their own without any form of human interference.

For the layperson, we are familiar with the term "artificial intelligence." It is the stuff of countless science fiction movies. However, few people understand that it is no longer science fiction but is definitely emerging in the realm of reality.

To explain:

- Deep learning is a form of machine learning that is used to teach machines how to learn in a way that is similar to the learning process in the human brain.

- Machine learning is a series of algorithms that give machines the ability to collect data, analyze it, and make decisions based on that analysis.

- Artificial intelligence is a machine programmed with machine learning, so it can gather data and make decisions based on that data.

In its most basic of forms, deep learning is simply another type of machine learning. Basic machine learning has improved over the years and deep learning is the latest link in the evolutionary chain. In its early stages of development, deep learning machines were only capable of learning from data that had already been labeled and stored into the machine. This meant it could only function with human supervision. Unsupervised learning was still far into the future, but many believed it was a very real possibility. Now, machines can learn in all sorts of ways.

How a Machine Learns

When it comes to learning, we humans do it without any thinking or programming. Our minds have never had to be trained in how to learn something. From the time we're born, our five senses go immediately into action, collecting data and submitting it to our brains. Our brains process it, analyze it, and then make decisions based on it. If we're walking out at night, our brain automatically assesses the scene, determines a level of danger, and tells our feet to move faster. If we're watching a movie, our brain takes all that information in and determines whether we should cry, laugh, or be angry. We have what is called unsupervised learning. No one has to program those details and responses into us.

In addition, once we learn a concept, it then becomes a foundation from which we can build on. We first learn the alphabet (the initial concept) then we learn the sounds related to that alphabet, then we learn to string sounds together, creating words. Eventually, we'll be able to read and this is called layered learning. With that thought in mind, we can continue to build our knowledge base and grow from there.

The concept behind machine learning is similar. While it is a far cry from doing the amazing things that a human brain can do, its function is based on a similar set of situations. A massive set of neural networks are created, each one communicating with the other. It also collects data and responds to the information it receives.

With artificial intelligence, the machine will be able to take in raw data and respond with a selection of pre-programmed responses. They will be able to "learn" from the data input and build on it. The major difference is that at present, machines can only learn from human input and develop their own concepts from the information gathered. This is one step closer to mimicking the human learning process.

Deep learning is basically a unique form of machine learning that is much more flexible than other previous forms used. By using a nested hierarchy of concepts, it can access many layers of non-linear information processing and achieve both supervised and unsupervised learning, which is ideal for pattern analysis and classification.

Deep neural networks consist of several layers called a hierarchal neural network. In this type of network, every layer has the ability to change its input data into something that is more abstract. The output layer will then combine the various features of input data and formulate a prediction. This method improves calculations, so it is much easier to understand.

While there are several different ways that machines can learn information, their strategies can be categorized into two separate classes. The first being supervised learning that uses labeled data to classify information. This form of learning is based on data that produces "expected answers." For example:

- Visual Recognition

  Imagine an AI designed to identify pedestrians walking across a street. It can be trained by inputting millions of short videos of street scenes collected. Some of the videos will have pedestrians walking while other videos will not. Some of the videos will have many people walking while some may have only one.

  With a number of learning algorithms applied to the data, each giving the machine access to the correct answers a variety of models are designed to teach the machine how to identify pedestrians in fast-moving scenes. The algorithms are tested against an unlabeled set of data that will check for accuracy.

- Predictions

  Supervised learning can also be used in making different predictions. A machine can be taught to estimate risk by inputting a large number of actual trades made by real investors and the results they received. It can then be asked to give an estimate of risk for each trade based on several fundamental factors of previous trades: price, volume, company, etc.

  It then takes its estimated risk and compares it to the historical results during several different time intervals (day, week, month, and year) to determine if its predictions are accurate or within normal expectations.

Unsupervised learning works a little differently. The machine receives input without any related yield factors. The answers are derived purely from the calculations made. The goal of this type of learning is to demonstrate the basic structure or dissemination of the information so that the machine can gather even more details about the information. Unlike with supervised learning, the machine is not given any right answer and there is no human instructor guiding its data. The AI may collect the data and sort it according to its similarities or differences even if there is no classification. The goal is to show a fundamental structure in the information in an effort to get a better understanding of it.

It is referred to as unsupervised learning because there is no instructor guiding it to the right conclusions. The machine will perform its own calculations in an effort to determine the nature of the data that it has collected.

While there are obvious advantages to unsupervised learning, there are still some problems it has yet to resolve. For example, a machine may be capable of identifying basic visual images (it can tell a cat from a dog) it may also end up creating new classifications in an attempt to distinguish between varying differences within a certain classification. (It may not be able to tell a German shepherd from a Chihuahua). Its purpose is to find relationships within the data it receives but this can create several problems when it tries to go further than that.

Clustering is when the AI attempts to decipher different groups within the data whereas association is an attempt to determine specific rules that will describe the data. Both of these can present huge problems in AI when their results are skewed by unanticipated groupings.

In reinforcement learning, the machine is trained to recognize activities. To come to this conclusion, it learns from its own actions and not from a human instructor giving it the necessary input. The goal, in this case, is not to make a classification or a prediction of events but instead to develop a policy of behavior.

We can find a perfect example of this in our relationship with household pets. If you're going to teach your dog a new trick, you can't just input the information and give it instructions on how you want it to behave. However, if you reward it for doing something and penalize it for other actions, eventually the dog will learn how to do the things that give it rewards and avoid the behavior and those actions that bring on discipline.

Reinforcement learning in machines works in a similar way with a few differences.

- Substitute the pet with the machine

- Substitute the treat for a reward function

- Substitute the good behavior with a resultant action

In order for this to work, you need to have a feedback loop that will reinforce what the machine is actually learning. It is rewarded when it performs certain actions and is disciplined when it is wrong. You might wonder how you can reward or discipline a machine that has no feelings and no emotions. The system will work something like this:

- The machine is given an internal state that it must maintain. This state is used to learn about their environment.

- The reward function is used to teach the machine how to behave.

- The environment is the situation or scenario that the machine must operate in. It consists of all the things the agent can observe and respond to.

- The action is the behavior of the machine.

- The agent performs all the deeds.

Let's apply this to the computer game, Mario. As the machine attempts to play the game it has an environment that allows it to perform many different functions. It does not know what will happen when it performs each of these functions. It can't see the entire environment at a single time, so it must navigate through the environment and make decisions on what to do. If it makes a move that will not advance it, then it is "punished" by not allowing it to move further. If it makes a move that advances it through the environment, it is "rewarded." In time the machine will learn exactly how to navigate safely through its environment until it reaches the conclusion of the game.

This is a very basic explanation of reinforcement learning but it should be enough to give you a general idea of how it works in machine learning. This form of unsupervised learning is not completely without human input. Someone has to create the environment that the machine will operate in as well as the consequences of each move. However, many are looking at this type of machine learning as the true future of artificial intelligence.

There are many applications and uses for machine learning and deep learning by extension that go far beyond the obvious. Already these learning mechanisms are being used in anomaly detection, human genome projects, sequencing analysis, crime analysis, and climatology among countless other uses and no doubt, there will be more practical applications that will be discovered in the future.

Chapter 3:
Understanding Neural Networks

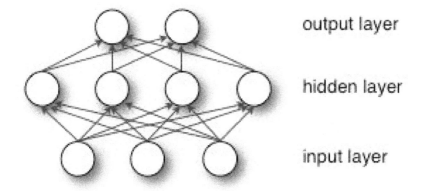

output layer

hidden layer

input layer

A s we've already learned, deep learning is reliant on the use of neural networks. These networks have been designed with the human brain in mind and if you compare a diagram of the brain with one of an artificial neural network (ANN), you will see some strong similarities.

What is a Neural Network?

Basically, a neural network can be described as a system patterned to operate like the human brain. The artificial neural network (ANN) is made up of layers of interconnected neurons that can receive a series of inputs and weights. It will take the data and perform a series of mathematical computations to come up with an output or result that can be similar to that of the biological brain.

A neural network is comprised of four components:

- Neurons

- Topology – this is the connective path between the different neurons

- Weights

- Learning Algorithm

While the function of an ANN is to mimic the human brain, it cannot do so exactly. One of the reasons for this is because the ANN is designed with thousands of neurons whereas the human brain consists of billions. So, there is the possibility that it will learn in a similar way to copy the human mind, but it is far from a perfect replication of the real deal.

The Structure of a Neural Network

Still, there are many functions that an ANN can perform that can be applied in a number of ways. Let's take a look at a diagram of a biological neuron found in a human brain and compare it.

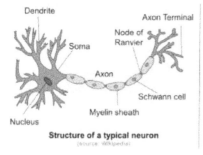

Structure of a typical neuron
(source: Wikipedia)

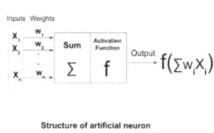

Structure of artificial neuron

In a biological neural network, the neurons consist of a cell nucleus that can receive input from the billions of other neurons in the network. This is done through a series of input terminals called dendrites (a group of dendrites together is referred to as a dendrite tree, which receives different types of signals from other neurons in the network. The signals can be excitatory or inhibitory in nature and are delivered via an electrochemical exchange of neurotransmitters.

How strong these input signals are will depend on several factors including the amplitude of the action coming from the previous neuron and the conductivity of the ion channels that are feeding the dendrites. The ion channels allow for the flow of electrical signals passing through the neuron's membrane or outer shell.

When signals are frequent or are of a larger magnitude, they generally have a much better conductivity in the ion channels so the signal is easier to propagate.

Depending on the type of signal received, the neuron will respond with either a message to activate or to inhibit. In other words, it will be told to turn on or turn off. Each neuron contains an electrochemical threshold, which determines whether the data received is sufficient enough to turn on the neuron or not. The result of all this activity is then sent to other neurons and the process continues.

Learning with the human brain is achieved by making tiny little adjustments to an existing configuration of neurons. Each configuration is created based on specific details before any learning can begin. How strong the connection of the neurons are, or the weights, are not random nor does the brain's topology have an effect on them.

Over time though, the strength of these connections will change based on their adjusting formation that affects both the topology and weights. Each time an adjustment is made learning happens. In the human brain, all of this happens automatically, in an instant. We watch this in babies as they learn to walk, talk, and play. Throughout our lives, we meet and get to know new people and our brains are capable of distinguishing one person from another based on numerous factors. The way they look, how they sound, their walk, etc. Every time we learn something new our brain makes these small adjustments to the neural networks and the results are stored as memories.

This function is completed in all sorts of tasks and environments. We can recognize objects, process sounds, and speech patterns. None of these skills are learned automatically but are developed slowly and repeatedly over extended periods of time. Each time the brain literally rewires itself to perfect the task it has been challenged to do.

Evidence of this was discovered through a series of experiments on animals. Their eyes were forced to remain closed for two months during their developmental stage while researchers observed the changes in the animal's visual cortex. After the two months, the animal's eyes were allowed to open but they were no longer receptive to light. In the cells and in the brain the eye had physically changed and was no longer able to function. We've now seen the same thing happening in humans. Studies have revealed that those who spend the majority of their lives in cities are found to be more sensitive to parallel lines and sharp edges, whereas those who spend the majority of their time in rural areas have eyes that are more sensitive to smooth textures.

How Learning Happens in ANNs

In artificial neural networks, the training starts with a fixed topology specifically chosen to address a certain problem. These topologies do not change with time and their weights are adjusted at random. This is done with the use of an optimization algorithm used to map the formation of input stimuli into a single cluster in order to get the desired result.

However, it is possible for ANNs to learn or to be fine-tuned based on their pre-existing representation. The process involves making adjustments to the previous weights from its original topology. This process does not happen as quickly as the human brain does but it does so at a very slow learning weight as it reacts to the newly supplied input data.

This training occurs when the weight update process starts to send data through the neural network. It measures the outcome and adjusts the weights according to the results. The weights are generally "pushed" in the direction that is most likely to improve the performance of the objective. So, an ANN designed to recognize objects will take the feedback and adjust the weights accordingly. This type of programming can be compared to a child who is learning how to recognize certain things. It is more a trial and error approach. After each failed attempt, his brain will analyze the feedback, and then take a different direction the next time.

This will be repeated until the child reaches the desired result. An ANN works the same general way. It is first given stimuli or data that has a known response along with a learning regime that will make adjustments in an attempt to maximize accuracy.

Once the machine has learned, it can then use the experience and apply it to new stimuli, even if it is something it has never been exposed to before. The more problems the machine has to solve, the faster it will be able to learn how to tackle new ones because the connections will become much more defined.

The More Exposure – The Better

While up until recently we weren't able to explain it scientifically, we have known for centuries that the more you expose a child to the world, the faster they learn. This is true, even when the learning process is an unpleasant experience. In fact, when the learning process is painful, the feedback they receive is even more memorable. With an ANN the same could be true. When an ANN is exposed to a variety of stimuli, the fine-tuning process can ensure that it is not being overly exposed to a single thread of processing.

With each additional type of stimuli, the network can "learn" how to classify new stimuli it will receive in the future. The basic principle behind this is based on the "Black Swan Theory," in the human brain and in ANNs if they have only been exposed to one type of stimuli it is impossible for them to conceive of another type of stimuli. For centuries, people had concluded that all swans were white because there had been no recorded facts of a swan of any other color. In other words, no one had seen or been exposed to a swan that was not white. However, later a Dutch explorer by the name of Willem de Vlamingh actually saw a group of black swans in Western Australia. Once he was exposed to this new stimuli, he had to adjust his understanding and create a new element of classifying them. If an ANN is only fed a limited stream of input, it cannot learn to classify other data that it has not been exposed to.

Its ability to draw knowledge from what it has learned is a huge stride in computer science. It allows machines to solve problems across all spectrums with a phenomenal array of applications, often with the ability to find a better solution than what would normally be achieved.

While this is a major advancement that far surpasses anything that machines have been able to do before, it is safe to conclude that this type of technology is still in its early stages. They still have a long way to go before they are capable of even coming close to being able to do what the human brain can do. Their topology is much too basic, they're learning algorithms are as of now, extremely naïve.

Still, as technology continues to advance, ANNs will continue to learn how to solve problems more effectively and face many more unknown issues in the future. Already these devices have been able to outperform human analysts in accuracy and speed in a number of areas. It is believed that one day, they will be able to multi-task like humans and mimic some of the most impressive human minds in all manner of things. But that goal is now many years in the future.

Input, Hidden, and Output Layers

Now, let's look a little closer at how these neural networks work. Even someone who is not computer savvy understands that computers use processors and memory to perform complex computations. For years, man has been astounded by the speed at which these machines can calculate a result. This has been going on for decades with huge success. Think of your calculator you carry around with you all the time. Computation is a given in the world of machines. But now, because of the introduction of neural networks, a whole new approach to problem-solving has begun.

To understand this better, we must first know that a computer consists of 10^9 transistors with a switching time of 10^9 seconds. What does that mean? Transistors are tiny little switches that are triggered by electrical impulses. These are the basic building blocks used in microchips and other computer devices. Compare that to the human brain, which has 10^{11} neurons, but they have a switching time of only 10^3 seconds.

The neurons in the human brain can be compared to the human nervous system, which has three different parts. The primary part is the brain or the nerve center, which is constantly receiving input it needs to process before making decisions. Input is received and sent to the nerve center, which processes all the data, analyzes it, and sends out instructions to the rest of the body.

- Data is received from the 5 senses.

- The central nervous system analyzes it and sends out instructions on how to respond.

- The body receives instructions from the brain and executes the appropriate action.

Now let's make another comparison with the machine to see how input differs. In a human brain:

- Synapses are at the most basic level and are completely reliant on molecules and ions for their actions.

- A neural microcircuit assigns a group of neurotransmitters to perform a particular operation

- The neural microcircuits are collected together to create subunits found in the dendrite trees

- Each neuron is capable of holding several of these dendrite subunits.

- These neural groupings work together to perform instructed operations.

- Interregional circuits create pathways, topographic maps of the cerebrum.

- The sensory system is the point where the topographic maps interrupt certain forms of conduct.

What is an Output Layer?

At the opposite end of the spectrum, a layer sits at the highest-level building block of the deep learning world. It is basically a container that receives the input and then adapts it with many of the non-linear functions and then passes the results on to the next layer. Layers are usually uniform in structure and can hold only one type of activation. This makes it easy to compare that layer to another part of the same network.

To make this easier to understand think of the first layer as the input layer and the last layer as the output layer.

What is a Unit?

A unit can be found in both input and output layers. It is simply the activation function where the inputs are adjusted using a nonlinear format. In most cases, a unit will have a number of income connections as well as some outgoing connections.

These neural networks calculate the weighted sum of all of the input, adjusts for bias, and then determines whether the data justifies factoring it in the decision or not. This decision is determined by checking the value that a neuron produces before it decides if an outside connection should be included as to whether it should be "turned on" or not.

Units are extremely complex, and a single unit can have numerous activation functions in it. The neurons contained in any given layer can receive similar functions or enactment work. The type of enactment utilized will be consistent across that specific layer.

Hidden Layers

A neural network consists of a massive number of artificial neurons (the units) that are stacked up in a series of layers. All of these neurons are interconnected through an extremely complex web. We've already discussed the input layer, which makes up the foundation of the entire network and the output layer, which performs the calculations and adapts the data to get a result. But there is most likely a number of hidden layers that lie between input and output layers.

Each neuron located in a hidden layer is also fully connected to all of the neurons in the previous layer as well as all the neurons in the following layer. It is only the input layer that does not need to modify the data received. Its sole responsibility is to receive the data from the environment. In essence, it is purely an information layer.

The hidden layer, however, must copy that data and distribute it to all the nodes it is connected to within the structure where it will perform the calculations needed to determine what to do with the information received.

The output layer performs any computations and then transmits instructions to the external environment.

Types of Neural Networks

There are several types of neural networks depending on when they were created and the extent of their complexity. The oldest of these neural networks and the simplest is the perceptron. The machine introduced in 1958, was capable of learning by means of input vectors assigned to different classes of data.

Every piece of data received has to be scaled up or down based on how important it is to the task. When a signal comes in, it is first multiplied by a predetermined weight value. So, if a neuron receives three different inputs, then that neuron will have three weights assigned to it; each can be adjusted individually.

When the computer is learning, the computer will determine the weight value based on the number of errors it made from its last test.

Next, these modified input signals are summed up to create a single value for each of the neurons. An additional computation is performed call the "bias" and is also added to the sum. After the machine learns, all the weights and biases shift so that the next result will be a little bit closer to what is the expected output demonstrating that it has actually learned from the exercise.

In the final phase, the result of the calculations is transformed into an output signal, which is then fed to the activation function and sent out to the external environment.

In perceptron, this is a very basic binary function that can produce only two possible results.

$$f(x) = \{1 \text{ if } w \cdot x + b > 0, 0 \text{ otherwise}\}$$

Based on this formula, the function will result in a 1 if the input is positive but if the input is negative, the return will be 0. Any neuron with a function like this one is a perceptron.

To train a perceptron requires the use of several preparation tests and determining the yield for each one. After each test is completed, the weights are rebalanced in a path so that it will reduce the yield error.

Adaline

The Adaline neural network (ADAptive LINear Element) followed perceptron. The general rule with Adaline sometimes called the delta rule is designed to minimize the number of output errors using a gradient descent.

After a training pattern has been completed, the weights are corrected in proportion to the error percentage. The primary difference between Adaline and perceptron is the way the output applies the learning rule. In perceptron, it uses the output of the threshold function learning. However, with ADALINE, it uses the output values of -1 or +1.

The delta rule states that for a given input vector, the output vector must be compared to the correct answer. If the difference is zero, the machine did not learn. If the zero is anything else, the weights need to be adjusted as an effort to lower the difference.

The delta rule makes use of the difference between the target output values and the obtained activation. In simple terms, it compares the desired output values of the machine with the obtained activation to determine learning. It disregards perceptron's threshold activation function and instead uses a linear sum of products to calculate the activation function of the output neuron.

Throughout the training process, the strength of the connections within the network is adjusted to reduce the difference between the two values. The reason for the shift was because the threshold activation function used with perceptron could not be used in gradient descent learning needed in programs that followed. The adjustment of the values at the end of each lesson could not get progressively closer to the target with this method. However, the linear activation used with Madeline made room for error calculations to yield outputs that could be adjusted with each lesson.

How do Algorithms Work?

There is a basic principle that applies to all supervised machine learning algorithms that allow them to perform predictive modeling. The focus of each algorithm is to take the target function (f) and create a map that takes the machine from the input variable (x) to the output variable (y). The resulting algorithm will look like this:

$$Y - f(x)$$

In this basic algorithm, the task is to make predictions about the future (y) with examples of input variables (x).

While this formula looks on the surface to be very simple, it becomes extremely complicated when you do not know the form of function f. If this variable was known, there would be no need for the machine to learn it. Instead, it would use it in the formula to get the desired result.

There is another element that makes performing this calculation even more complicated. The algorithm must also allow for errors (e) that are completely independent of the input data (x), so the formula must be adjusted.

$$Y = f(x) + e$$

There are a number of variables that could represent e. The machine may not have enough attributes to characterize the best mapping solution. With this type of error, no matter how good the machine is at making estimates, it will never be able to reduce that error.

Algorithms like these make it possible for machines to learn and to make predictions. This is termed "predictive analytics." In general, machine learning algorithms are designed to estimate a mapping function of several output variables when they are applied to the given input variables.

With these algorithms, the machine can learn to make different assumptions based on the formula of its underlying function. If the machine does not have enough data to generate a reasonable assumption, it will not be able to learn no matter how well it performs its programmed tasks. Without algorithms carefully designed to target the task at hand, machine learning would not be what it has become today.

Chapter 4:
Presentation of Deep Learning

While the primary purpose of deep learning is applied to ANNs, its development has many more applications where it can be used. Since scientists first realized how many different ways these neural networks can be applied, research has begun in a wide range of areas creating systems that go far beyond the artificial.

These new and innovative machines represent the future of deep learning and are expected to eventually replace the artificial neural networks in use today.

This is a phenomenal accomplishment in the history of mankind, however, as advanced as they are, they still have many limitations; one being their immense size. They require many systems in order for them to function properly but their list of tasks they can perform is very small. Think of it in terms of the first computers invented. They were large in size (some taking up an entire room) but the number of functions they could perform was actually quite limited.

The same could be said for these deep learning machines today. The goal for the future is to create a type of artificial intelligence that requires only minimal human input and can perform a vast number of functions. This was the underlying purpose of deep learning.

The deep neural network is the next evolutionary step of the ANN. The machines used are considerably smaller but with the capability of performing even more complex functions that go far beyond the capabilities of the ANNs. Deep neural networks are targeted to have a more usable program that will allow the machines to work effectively and efficiently without consuming so much space and energy.

To achieve this deep neural network of the future, several things had to change.

GPUs/CPUs

Most of us are familiar with CPUs (central processing units). We may not know exactly what it is, but we know it represents the brains of our personal computer systems. For years, the CPU was both the heart and the brain of the computer.

In time, however, the CPU was improved upon with the aid of another computer part that was not so familiar. The graphics processing unit or the GPU. In every computer, there are chips responsible for displaying images on the computer monitor and a GPU is one of the most powerful chips you have. While these chips have the same function, some are not as effective as others. Some will provide only the most basic of graphics and others will function on a much higher level.

The GPU is one of those components of your computer which goes much further than displaying a clear picture of a computer game. Their role does not stop at displaying graphics, they can be programmed and perform computations separate from the CPU in any system. Deep learning uses GPUs to address many of the limitations that the ANNs have faced since their inception.

For the most part, GPUs were initially designed for use in computer games but because of their immense power they have far exceeded expectations and have quickly been adapted for other uses that have been applied in a number of ways.

How is the GPU Designed?

To get better graphics on your computer, you need a better graphics card, a basic truth that most people can readily understand. At its most basic level, a GPU differs from a CPU in that while they perform basically the same function but with entirely different architectures. Both machines will receive a problem in the form of zeros and ones (binary code) and both will solve the problem quickly.

However, the way they are designed is where they part ways. CPUs are designed with hundreds of simple cores and GPUs have thousands. When you compare this difference in computers you can understand it more clearly. The top of the line computer, the Mac Pro, has a six-core processor while the NVidia GTX 980 graphics card has more than 2000. This allows for clearer pictures, better resolution, and a host of other benefits.

There are other differences beyond having more core. You can think of the CPU as a device that can perform lots of easy tasks that it can complete quickly and efficiently. On a computer system, it can solve geometrical equations or shade in a picture. The GPU, on the other hand, is better suited for complex tasks and problem-solving. This is why it is so much more practical to use with artificial intelligence.

Today's advanced neural networks make use of a number of systems to keep them running including algorithms and GPUs. As a result, deep learning can be adapted to all sorts of industries to help solve many problems that may or may not apply to artificial intelligence. It is already being used in speech recognition, language processing, and computer vision.

Because GPUs are a major component of machines, it can be adapted to a wide variety of situations using many layers of data to solve a host of problems. Depending on the different designs and strategies used, GPUs can help in three different classifications of deep learning.

- **Unsupervised or Generative Learning**

  This type of learning is meant to capture obvious images for pattern analysis at times when no target data is available.

- **Supervised Deep Learning**

  These are used to discern and classify different patterns.

- **Hybrid Deep Networks**

  These are designed to distinguish between different elements in the data. The objective of hybrid deep networks can be improved when used with supervised learning and are primarily used to analyze different parameters in the input data.

Deep Learning Methods

Another aspect of deep learning is something called Dynamic Programming. This allows the machine to tackle certain problems with the use of algorithms based on a recurrent formula and a starting state. A "state" is a way to describe a particular situation or problem the machine must solve. A sub-solution is then constructed from any previously found ones in the system. DP algorithms are a fundamental part of the framework in neural networks and graphical models.

- **Unsupervised Learning with SL & RL**

  This deep learning method is regularly used when encoding input data is needed. Data streams like video or speech need to be encoded into a form that is better geared towards machine learning. These codes describe the initial data in a manner that reduces redundancy, so it can be fed into SL or RL machines. These machines usually have a much smaller search space and cannot manage such large qualities of raw data.

- **Back Propagation**

  This is simply a method that allows the system to compute the partial gradients of a function. When the machine solves an optimization problem with a gradient-based method, it must also compute the function each time it repeats. To compute the gradient, the machine can either use analytic differentiation: it knows the form of the function and simply needs to compute the derivatives, or it can use the approximate differentiation using finite differences.

- **Stochastic Gradient Descent**

This is a very intuitive way to create a gradient descent. Imagine looking at a river as it flows from the top of a mountain. The goal of the machine is to determine exactly where the river is going and the path it is going to take. To accomplish this the machine needs to know certain elements of the problem: the terrain of the mountain, lowest point of the foothill, the curvature of the hills. In machine learning, the input point (the very top of the hill) may be the only input it has to solve the problem. As it tries to work out the solution, it will label dips and valleys as local minima solutions, which it will have to navigate to get around. The output could be any number of possible paths the river might take. Each time it addresses this problem it may reach its final destination in a completely different manner each time.

- **Learning Rate Decay**

To improve on the Stochastic Gradient Descent, there is the Learning Rate Decay method. This method is often used to reduce the learning rate over a period of time. It allows the machine to make large changes at the start of a training test by using larger learning rate values and decreasing them according to the weights assigned in the training procedure. It may lower the learning rate based on the epoch or by using punctuated large drops at specific epochs.

- **Occam's Razor**

  This method works in the simpler problems rather than the complex. The concept of the possible solutions, the machine will select the date with the simplest explanation available. Given the input, the machine will determine a list of possible solutions to the problem. A good way to think of it is to imagine a patient going to the doctor complaining of a headache and a sore throat. There are several medical conditions that can explain a headache, a brain tumor, an aneurysm, a stroke. There are also several possibilities that can explain a sore throat, an infection or a virus. The machine would compare all of these solutions and filter out those that explain only one symptom and not both. Then it will finally filter out the conditions that are extreme and narrow it down to the simplest one. A cold or the flu would explain both symptoms.

There are many more methods that can be applied to deep learning. Because of their fast speeds and impressive computational power, they have been at the heart of machine learning for years. With these additions to machines, learning can be accelerated to work at least 50x faster.

Chapter 5:
Multilayer Perceptron

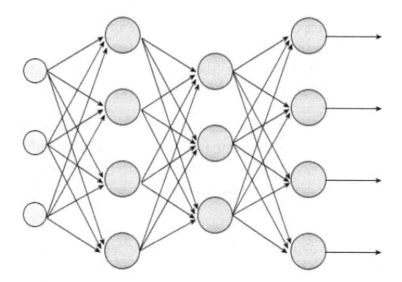

ultilayer Perceptron or MLP is normally used when the machine has access to standard data. This would be any type of data contained in a table format with rows and columns. The factors (rows and columns in these algorithms are interchangeable so the machine can switch a row for a column or vice-versa without having the change the value of the information it contains.

An MLP can take the input and change it using a learned non-linear transformation. The change can effectively project the input data into an area where it can be separated into layers.

The middle layer or the hidden layer is sufficient enough to create an MLP.

How it Works

When training MLPs there are a few things that must be kept in mind. First, there are a number of hyperparameters that cannot be enhanced or improved with gradient descent. So, finding these hyperparameters isn't a simple problem to solve. First, they can't be easily optimized nor can the machine apply gradient strategies to them. The trick is to find these hyperparameters in the neural network.

You can discern from its name that a Multilayer perceptron consists of more than one perceptron. They have an input layer that receives a signal, an output layer to make a prediction, and a varying number of hidden layers that will run the computations.

MLPs are usually used to solve supervised learning problems. They are trained with a set of input/output pairs and will model the dependencies that exist between the inputs and the outputs. During the training, adjustments are made to the weights and biases as it tries to reduce the error rate.

MLPs are considered feedforward networks and they work in a similar fashion to a game of tennis. They have two functions, which they switch back and forth. Each function is a guess and the next function is the answer. Since every guess represents a test of what they have assumed to be the correct answer the response is the feedback informing the machine that it is right or wrong.

With the forward pass, the signal moves from the input layer, cross the net (the hidden layers) to the output layer. When it hits the ground, it is measured and the truth is returned.

Backpropagation

There is another type of signal pass that is used with MLPs. It is called the backpropagation and it applies the chain rule of calculus, partial derivatives of an error function, along with the weights and biases. In this process, determining the differentiation between all the elements will produce a gradient or a landscape of different errors. That taken along with the parameters can be adjusted with each pass taking it one step closer to the minimum error percentage.

With MLP, the back and forth passes will continue until the machine reaches a point where it cannot get any lower. This is called the point of convergence.

To properly complete a backpropagation, three things are needed:

1. A data set in both input and output pairs where x is the input and y is the desired output.

2. Feedforward neural networks where the layers are all completely connected.

3. An error function that calculates the output of the input data given.

This type of neural network requires the machine to calculate the gradient of error with weights and biases for each pass until a solution is reached.

Applications

There are several applications where this type of machine learning can be very effective.

Function approximation where the network learns how to estimate the value of a particular function. Data is stored in the machine or fed to it and the system processes it to identify a pattern.

Time series prediction the network learns how to predict a value using data obtained during a specific time frame. This application is most often used in stock markets and similar fields where anticipating future moves are needed.

Language Processing machines learn to decipher spoken language with language modeling. The program uses deep learning networks and is capable of understanding native language in such a way that they can actually have basic conversations with participants. They can communicate rationally for extended periods of time. This application is so advanced that these machines are capable of understanding jokes, rephrasing expressions, and adapting to a wide range of verbal communications. You may have already used one of these applications. If you've ever used Google Translate online, you understand the concept.

Long/Short Term Memory Networks are used in backpropagation where the gradient signal is multiplied numerous times by the weight matrix. If the weights in a particular matrix are very small, it can result in a situation commonly referred to as vanishing gradients because the gradient signals can diminish to the point where the learning has slowed down so much that it cannot continue.

On the other hand, it can become so complex that the task can create long-term dependencies on the data. This can end up in a situation where the signal becomes so large that learning cannot be contained, and you end up with something referred to as exploding gradients.

These challenges are addressed with the use of the Long/Short Term Memory Networks, which utilize a new structure called the memory cell. This cell consists of four major components.

1. An input gate

2. A neuron that has a self-recurrent connection

3. A forget gate

4. An output gate

The neuron with the self-recurrent link comes with a weight of 1.0 and assures that the memory cell remains constant from one time to the next. The other gates modulate interactions that happen between the memory cell and the environment. The cell's input gate can allow a signal to enter and alter the status of the memory cell or block it altogether, but the output gate can permit the status of the memory cell to have an impact on other neurons on the network or block it from doing so. The role of the forget gate is to modulate the self-recurrent connection and allow the cell to forget its previous status if needed.

Chapter 6:
Convolutional Neural Networks

Convolutional neural networks use many types of identical copies of the same neuron. This makes it possible for the network to learn a neuron one time and then apply it in a number of different situations, thus simplifying the overall learning process and lowering the chance of machine error.

These systems were inspired by the biological processes found in the brains of living beings. It was made to mimic the design of the neurons in the visual cortex. In this type of neural network, individual cortical neurons respond to stimuli only within a limited visual field. Collectively, the visual field of many different neurons can efficiently cover the entire visual field.

CNN's are basically a way to classify neural networks that have already proved to be very powerful in specialized fields like image recognition and classification. These networks can identify faces, objects, and traffic signs by controlling how machines and self-driving cars see.

CNN's are made up of several different convolutional and sub-sampling layers all connected together. The input layer is represented by the formula:

$$m \times m \times r \text{ picture}$$

In this formula, the m is equal to the height and the width of a picture and r represents the number of color channels. The convolutional or the input layer will have k filters sized with the formula

$$n \times n \times q$$

With this formula, n is less than the dimensions of the image and q can be either equal or of a smaller size. This factor could shift with every filter. The number of filters allows for the ascent to any locally associated filters, including maps.

Maps can then be sub-sampled with a mean or max pooling that spreads out over a contiguous region using the formula

$$p \times p$$

In this case, p has to be a value between 2 and 5 depending on the size of the input.

Beyond the convoluted layers, there could be any number of connected hidden layers. These connected layers can be difficult to distinguish from the layers in a multilayer neural system.

In a CNN, each layer in the arrangement can change a single volume of activation through a differentiable function. The layers may be labeled as the convolutional or input layer, a pooling layer, and a fully connected layer. These layers could all be stacked to create a highly complex network.

Chapter 7:
How Deep Learning Can Be Used

With the growing emergence of artificial intelligence and deep learning, there is more than enough opportunities for this science to grow and expand beyond its present boundaries. There are three noteworthy events that have been instrumental in projecting this type of technology forward and into the world's consciousness.

The ability of machines to learn and be trained is an important significance for our future. As a result, the framework that has begun to overtake the traditional and outdated technologies in various fields has made it possible for humans to take immense strides in their progress. This can be great news for some people and may cause trouble for others, but the reality is that this technology is here to stay.

Still, like every other modern advancement in the world, people and businesses alike are now learning how to use deep learning to solve a host of real-world problems. However, there are fundamental elements in how deep learning is used and applied in these situations that cannot be ignored.

Pre-Training

In machine learning, the process does not focus on collecting numerous datasets. Rather, the machines do the exact opposite. When comparing deep learning techniques to other technological methods and at the same time it is important to establish a consistent measure that determines which strategy works better on the same or similar evaluation period, the general rule of thumb is to measure the performance of each strategy based on a set number of datasets using a regular evaluation period.

The problem with this is that in real-world situations, the result is not about how to get an extra percentage out of the error rate but is more focused on building a better robot so to speak. This means that labeling training strategies and highlighting which algorithm used can help the machine to learn better.

To solve many real-world problems, this can turn out to be a very expensive process.

For example, in the field of medicine, a machine designed to detect lymph nodes in the human body by analyzing tomography images (or CT scans) is already in use. This is an extremely time-consuming task because the machine must recognize very small structures. It can also be very expensive as well. Based on the assumption that a radiologist earns around $100/hr. and a CT scan can only produce 4 images an hour the cost of such a test could easily run up to $10,000 to get enough images for a proper diagnosis.

Add to that the consultation fee for having an additional doctor on hand to confirm the diagnosis, acquiring sufficient data to give an accurate diagnosis could easily go beyond the quarter of a million mark. That is just for diagnosis only; it does not include any treatment options that will come later.

Credit History

Deep learning is also used in determining your credit score. Machines can learn to analyze patterns to determine who has the highest risk of defaulting on their loan before credit is issued to them. Companies that issue loans to anyone are at the highest risk of finding someone who will default on their loan. This makes issuing credit a very expensive venture. Machines that can learn to analyze spending patterns, payment history, and financial health can make sure that those risks are greatly reduced.

In Computer Games

You've probably already heard about computers that have learned how to play chess or other games. In this type of learning, the pixels on the screen form the basis of the game. The goal and the most complicated task the machine must do is to break through the Deep Mind.

Depending on how complex the game is there are many elements to game playing that the computer has to learn. It will have to navigate through environments, different storylines, character behavior, and other rules in order to master the game.

With it comes to pre-training, the fine-tuning segment learns how to quantify different classes and make the necessary adjustments. Neural networks are pre-trained based on specified datasets and then are fine-tuned to fit within the parameters of a unique problem. Each problem has its own set of different anomalies. The input data informs the machine exactly which layer needs to be adjusted and the learning rates are reset, usually a little higher than the last layer.

In Education

The focus of education is to reach a point where you outperform learning models regardless of the model you choose. When functioning with real-world applications it is not always easy to design a model that functions as it should. It is important that when a learning machine makes an error that it can understand how and why it did so. It must have some ability to ascertain why a specific model did better than any other previous solution, and it is extremely important that you understand that the existing model in use cannot be tricked.

In the Movie Industry

Machine learning is now capable of adding sounds to silent video. The framework was designed to analyze 1000 examples of video playing with a drumstick beating on different surfaces to create different sounds. The machine then studies the video and compares it to a database of pre-recorded sounds and matches the right sound with the scene in the video. The finished scene was then tested for accuracy with humans who were asked to determine which video was the real silent film and which one was matched with sounds added in by computer.

Automatic Language Translation

This type of deep learning trains machines to identify spoken words, expressions, and sentences in an input language and then translate it into a target language. Automatic translation by machines is not a new application but deep learning has been able to add a whole new element to machine translating. It can now automatically translate written text both in printed form and handwritten form and it can also translate images.

Text translation is performed without the use of preprocessing, allowing the algorithms the freedom to learn from the interdependencies that exist between words and then mapping them to the target language.

This function is usually done with the convolutional neural networks because of their ability to identify and recognize all sorts of images. These machines can recognize letters in text, translate them, and then immediately send the translated text to its destination.

Images can also be translated by classifying objects in a photograph as a single set of known objects stored in its memory. Object detection includes being able to identify one or more objects in a photograph and drawing and labeling a box around them.

Handwriting Generation

Probably one of the most impressive applications of deep learning is the ability machines now have to produce handwriting. The machine learns by analyzing a collection of handwriting samples and then produces its own handwritten word or phrase. This is done by inputting a series of coordinates using a digital pen to create its own handwriting samples.

Once the machine has learned the images of samples, it studies the relationship that exists between the pen and the letters to create a new set of handwritten samples to choose from. This may not seem very amazing to you, but the machine can actually learn different handwriting styles and then mimic them back to you.

There are many more uses for deep learning that are in play today. Without your realizing it, you're coming in direct contact with deep learning machines every day. When you turn on your TV, when you make a purchase, use your credit, or even when you go out to eat. Deep learning has already permeated every part of human life and is poised to take us into a whole new era for the world. Ever wonder what deep learning has in store for the future?

Chapter 8:
Deep Learning and the Future

While deep learning is slowly making inroads into our everyday lives, there is much more of it in our future to look forward to. It is a rapidly growing form of technology and as a result, we can realistically expect to see much more of it in the years to come. It will continue to be integrated into ways we are familiar with but more importantly, in ways that we may not have yet thought of.

Considering what we already know about neural networks and the steady stream of research projects popping up all across the globe, we don't really need a machine that can learn to predict what the future holds. Perhaps everything we expect may not pan out, but we can be certain that whatever it is, someone, somewhere is already working on it. Let's take a look at some of the predictions others have made about the future of deep learning to see where we're going.

A Function for the General Population

Some expect that one-day deep learning and artificial intelligence will be available for the general population in much the same way as the personal computer is now in nearly every household. Already, people are working on using this technology to build smart homes that will anticipate your every need, self-driving cars are just one generation away, and computer technology that will anticipate your every move.

Its Ability Will Only Expand

The capabilities of deep learning will improve opening up even more doors to functions that will make life easier. No doubt deep learning can do amazing things today, but it is still a far cry from truly thinking like a human brain. As its technology and the science behind it grows, we can expect whole new forms of learning to be presented with models that will move away from the limitations it now holds. Today, deep learning is limited to recognition, classifications, computations, and identification. Eventually, it will be able to reason like the human mind and will be capable of abstract thinking as well. When that happens the implications that will follow will be immense.

They Will Have More Autonomy

Right now, all forms of deep learning need some involvement from humans to function. In supervised learning, the machine must be fed data and tested based on parameters set by humans. Even in unsupervised learning, these machines need some input from humans to start their program and utilize inputted data.

In the future, these machines could eventually reach the point where they can create the next generation of their technology themselves, program them completely without the aid of human interference. As they continue to learn and to store the information they have acquired, accessing it when needed, it is highly possible that this reusable knowledge will help them to design and create their own machine learning and adapt it to their own needs.

There Will be a Move Away from Models

Right now, a principal part of deep learning is the different models in existence. In the future, it is expected that the models we see in use today will one day become computer programs that will be able to adapt to all sorts of situations whether pre-programmed for it or not.

More Advancements in Medical Technology

It is feasible that every medical lab in the country will be equipped with learning machines that will be able to diagnose illnesses, test lab results, learn how to perform surgery, or dispense with medication, all without human interaction. Imagine a world where a machine can analyze your DNA samples to help doctors to learn about your potential for medical risks or to determine if you have a gene for Alzheimer's or some other illness. This knowledge would allow you to take steps ahead of time in order to stop the disease from ever happening.

Biomechanics

The future may also usher in a new era of biomechanics. Already nanotechnology is able to create limbs and other body parts for patient use. Instead of having to use a donor's heart, these tiny learning machines could be able to create a heart for you in a lab. An artificially created limb can be taught to perform like the real limbs would.

Better Mobile Technology

Can you make a smartphone any smarter? With deep learning, anything is possible. Mobile technology could literally become a personal virtual assistant, scheduling appointments, performing personal tasks, and managing your life overall. If you had the freedom away from such mundane chores you will then be free to engage in a host of other activities that you haven't been able to find the time for.

Machines Performing Mundane Tasks

One day, machines will perform the basic and more mundane tasks that humans now have to do. Self-driving trucks will come to your neighborhood will pick up your garbage every week, they will clean your home, prepare your meals, and even tidy up your home.

They Will Have Bigger Capabilities

As more algorithms are introduced, deep learning can only expand. This means there will be more automation, so each machine will be able to perform more than one task. Each layer of the neural networks can introduce a whole new feature to add to their abilities. In time, you'll have an AI that's sole responsibilities are to take care of you.

The reality is that we don't know exactly what the future holds or what to expect, but if history tells us anything, we all understand that this type of technology has a very long and prosperous future. We may not ever see the day when Sarah Conner has to fight off the Terminator and we are far from the threat of world domination by machines, but we can fully and realistically expect that machines will slowly become a major part of our lives.

We may not see it in our lifetime, but the time will come when machines will change the way live, work and play in a myriad of different ways. Every day, we are learning more about this new and exciting technology and what it can do for us. One thing for sure, our future looks bright and promising with deep learning on the horizon we have many good things to look forward to.

Conclusion

Living in today's modern age can be very exciting. We exist at a time that only a half-century ago was the stuff of science fiction. Today, with deep learning at the core of computer science we have the ability to do things never thought possible.

Whether you're reading this book out of curiosity or if you're seriously considering playing a significant role in the future of this new technology, we hope that we have been able to at least peak your interest in this subject and what it means for all of us.

We have made every attempt to keep the language simple enough for the layman to understand but technical enough not to bore those who have a base knowledge of the subject. Still, sad to say, we've only touched on the subject in these pages. Even though these few pages could not take you into the depths of the world of deep science we have been able to give you a basic overview of the subject and how it came about. We've talked about what foundation knowledge you need to get started.

You learned about neural networks, what they mean and how they work and some of the different types of networks and how they can be used in our modern and progressive world. Then we discuss the presentation of deep learning, multilayer perceptron's, and convolutional neural networks. All different aspects of the same technology.

No doubt, you have a lot to think about when it comes to deep learning. It is the technology that lies at the very heart of machine learning and artificial intelligence. These amazing programs, patterned after the human brain and the way it works are opening all sorts of new doors to the future. You don't have to be a scientist, mathematician, or a computer technician to see the possibilities. There is more than enough room to grow and whether you plan to work someday in this field or you're looking to use it in your personal life, this technology is introducing us to a completely new way of life.

We hope that by now, you understand how those ads keep popping up when you're searching the Internet, how Netflix knows exactly what movies you're going to like, or how that one company seems to find you wherever you go. You now understand how Google translate can translate languages in an instant and you understand how Twitter has the capacity to comprehend and analyze everything you post with them.

Deep learning is a very complex subject and it may be difficult to understand. If that's you, don't feel discouraged. Keep this book close by and read it in small bites. Eventually, you will grasp its meaning and if you're seriously interested, don't be afraid to reach out for more knowledge. Thank you for walking with us into the world of machine learning, artificial intelligence, and deep learning. We hope that you enjoyed it and will be ready to come back for more soon.

Finally, if you found this book useful in any way, a review on Amazon is always appreciated!